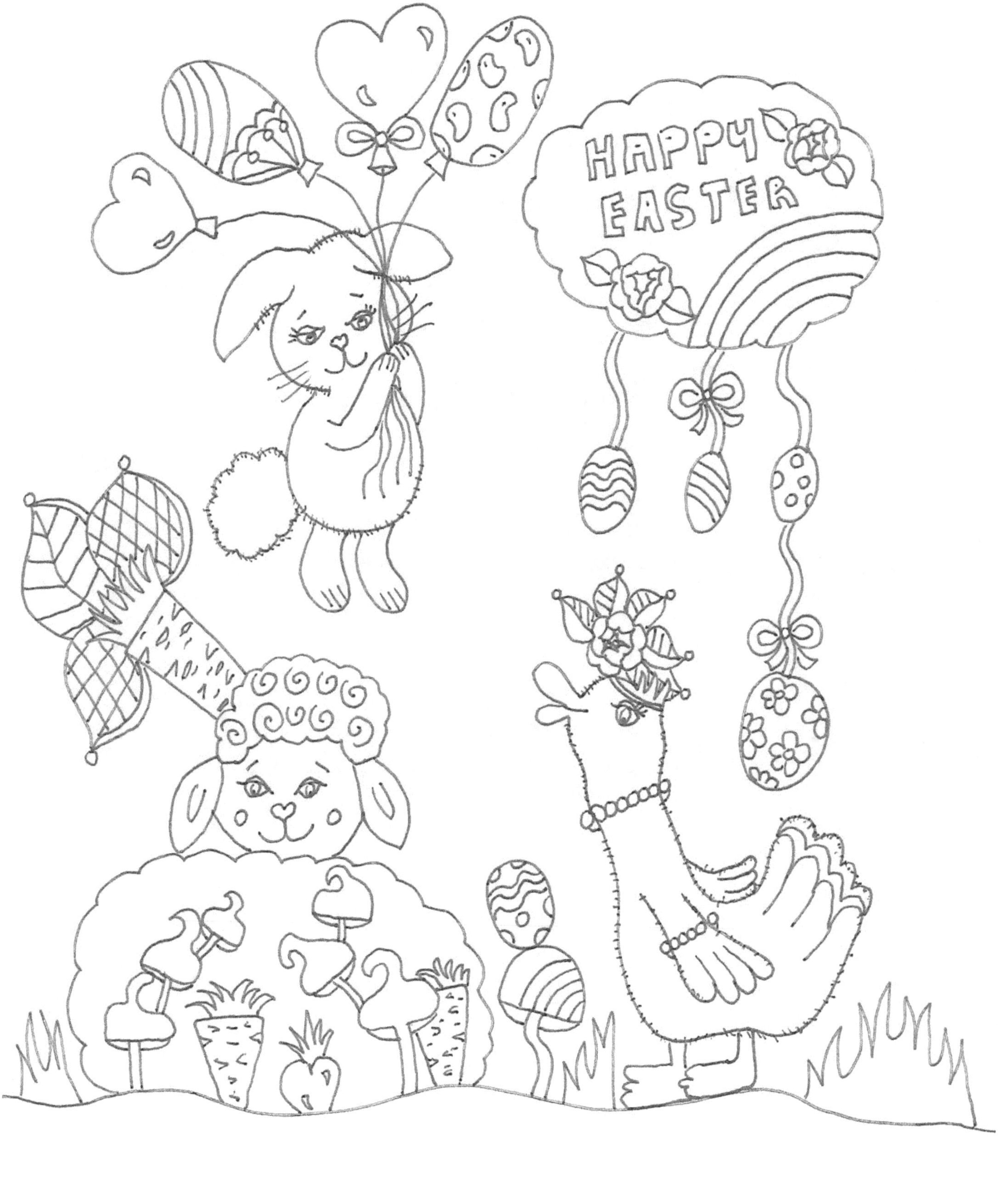

I0462611

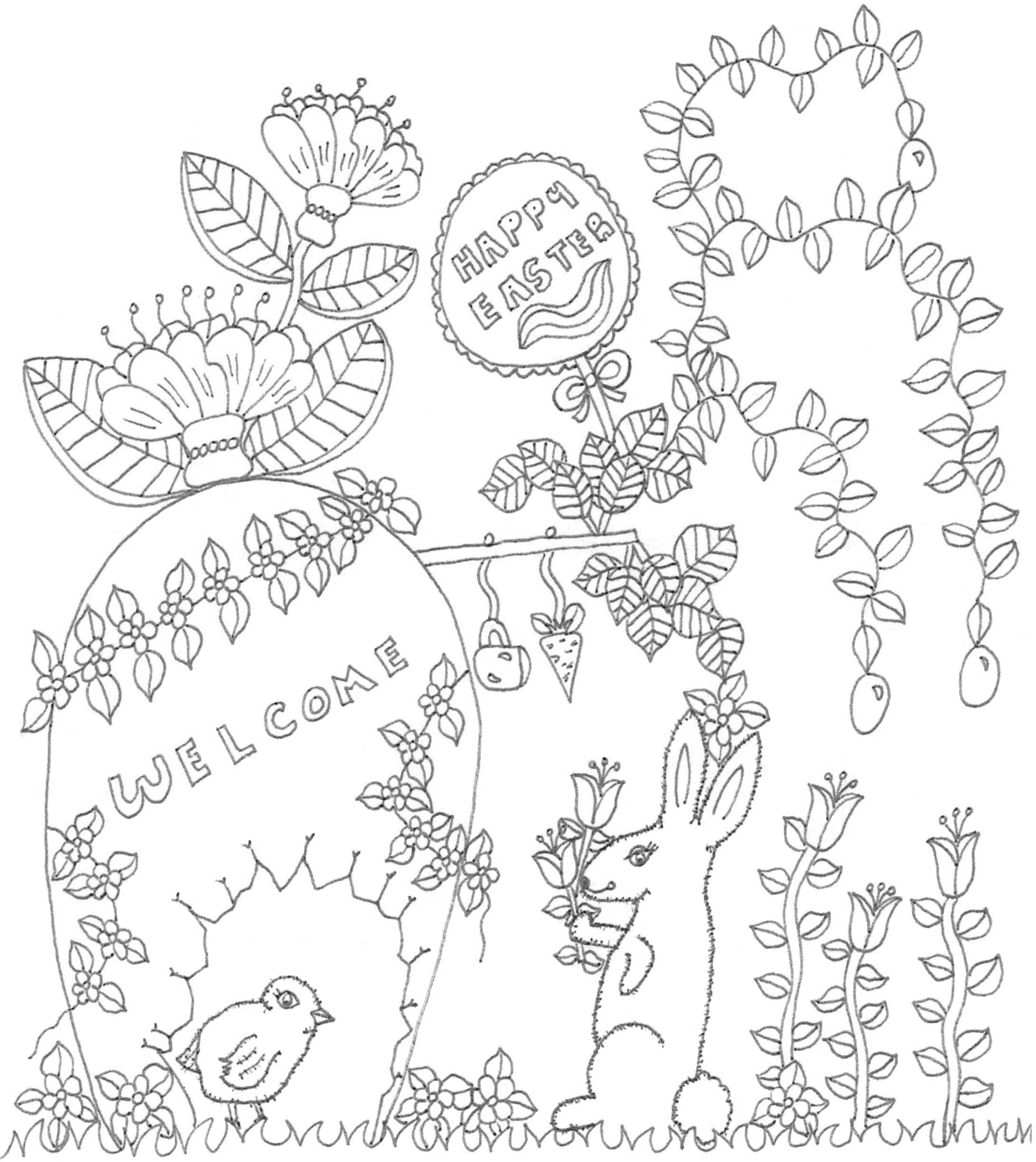
HAPPY EASTER
WELCOME

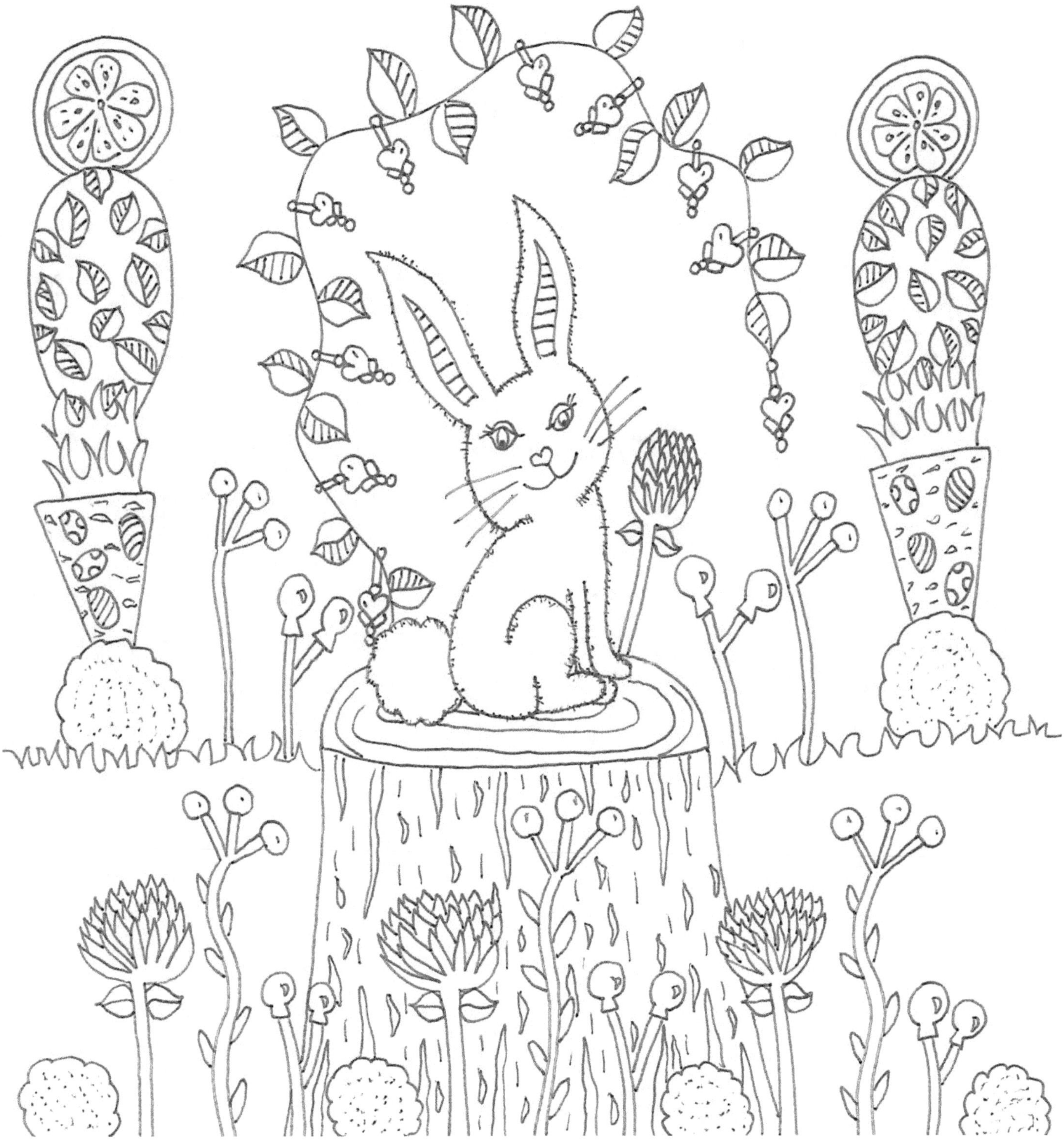

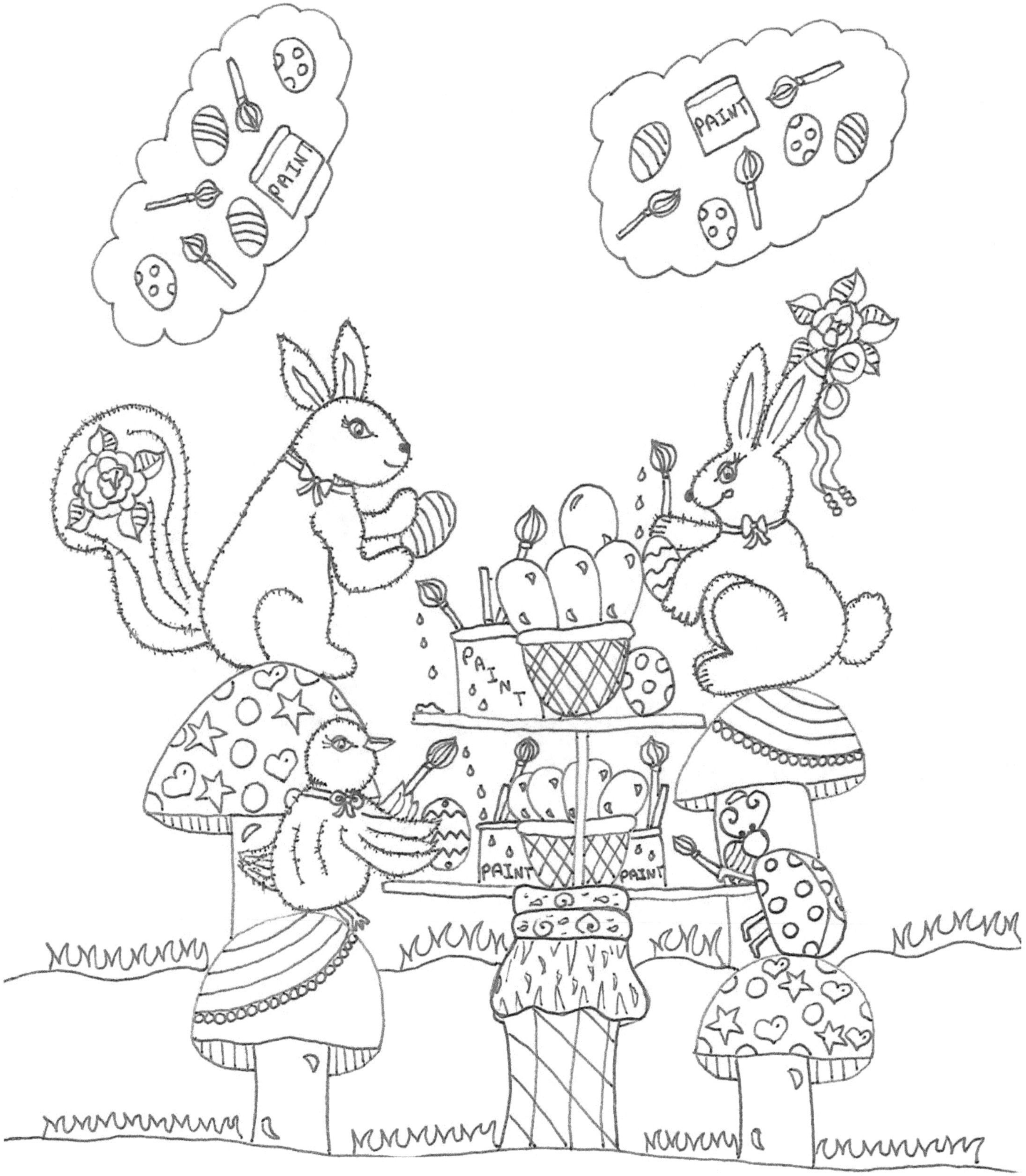
PAINT
PAINT
PAINT
PAINT
PAINT

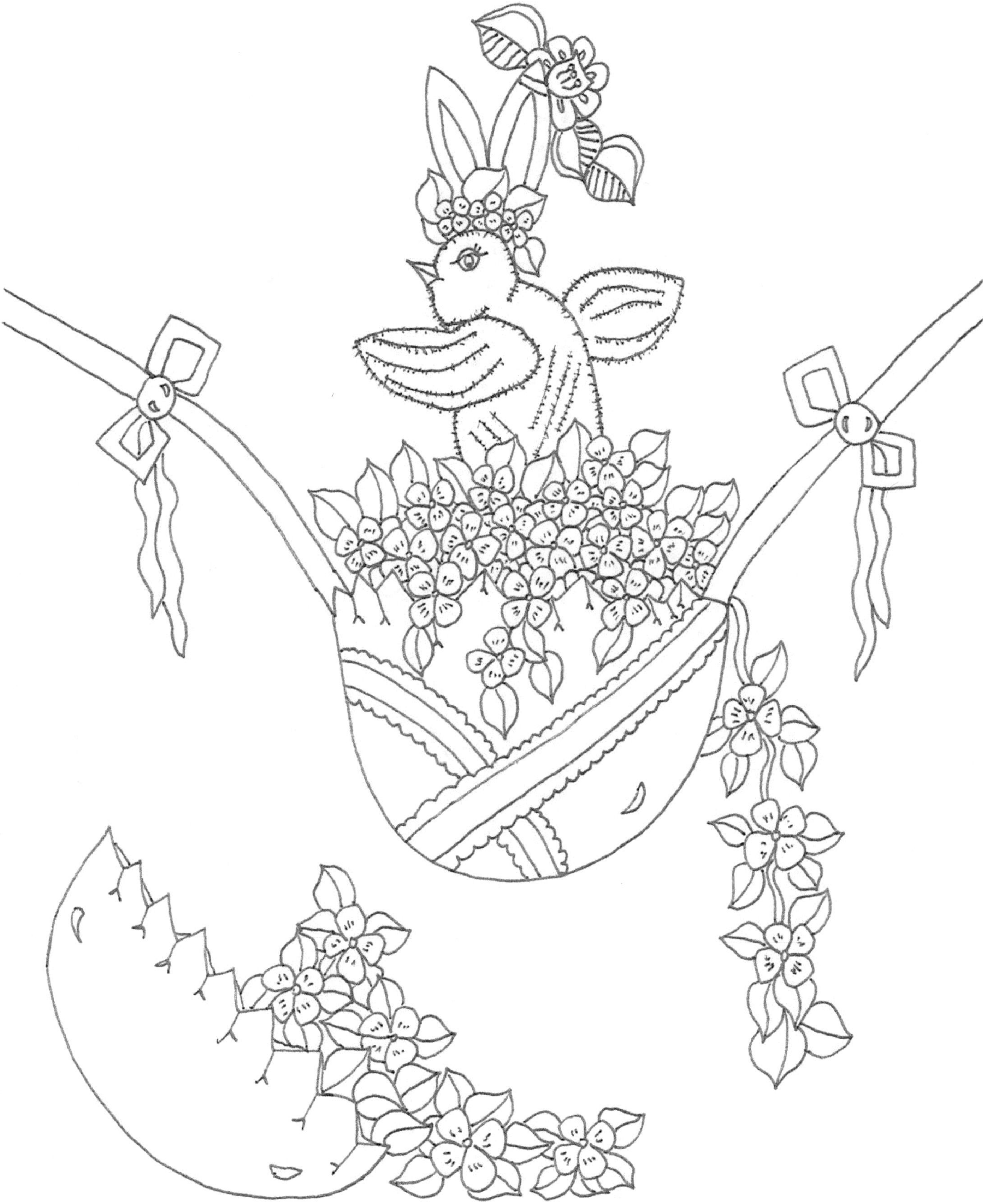

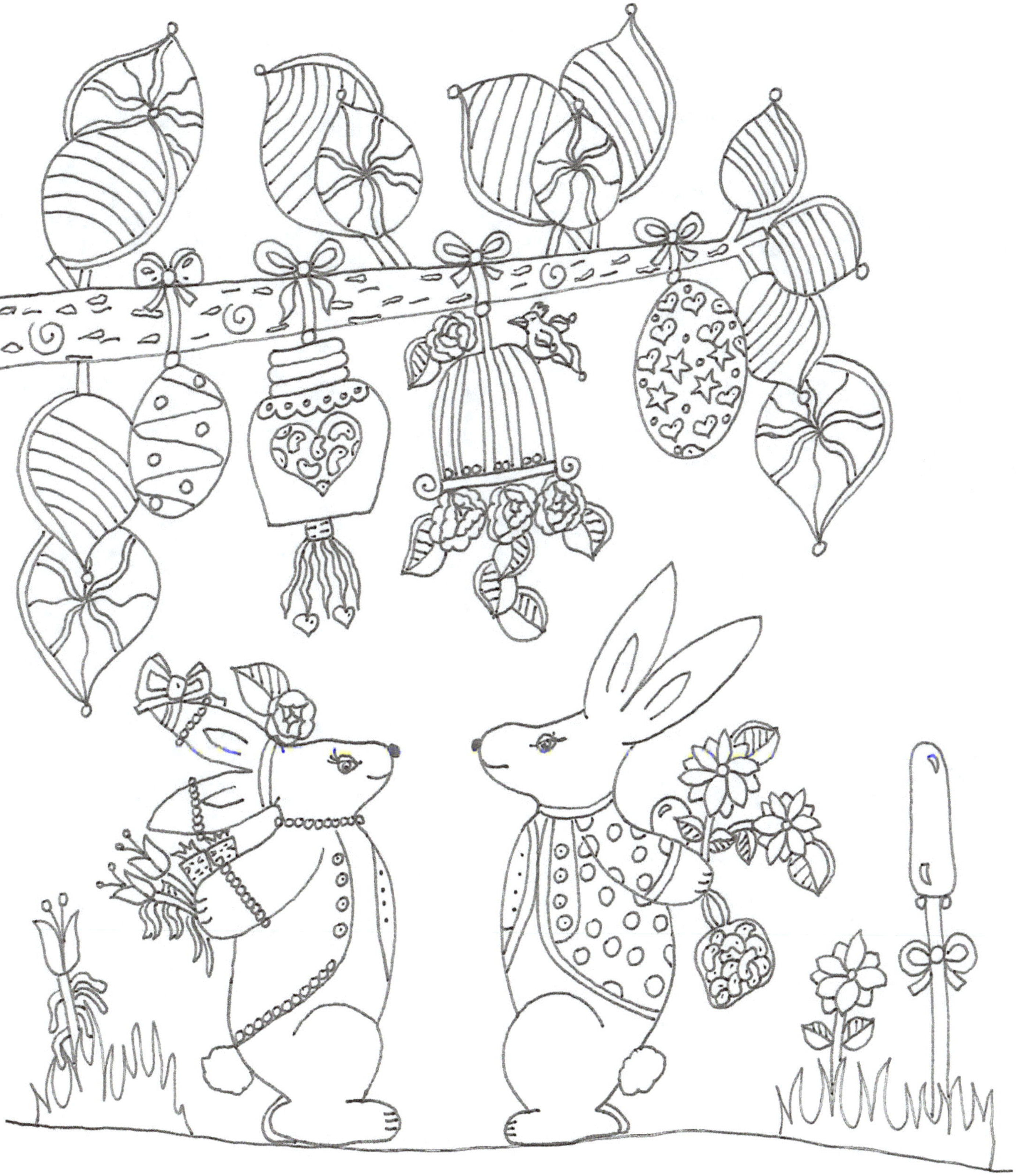

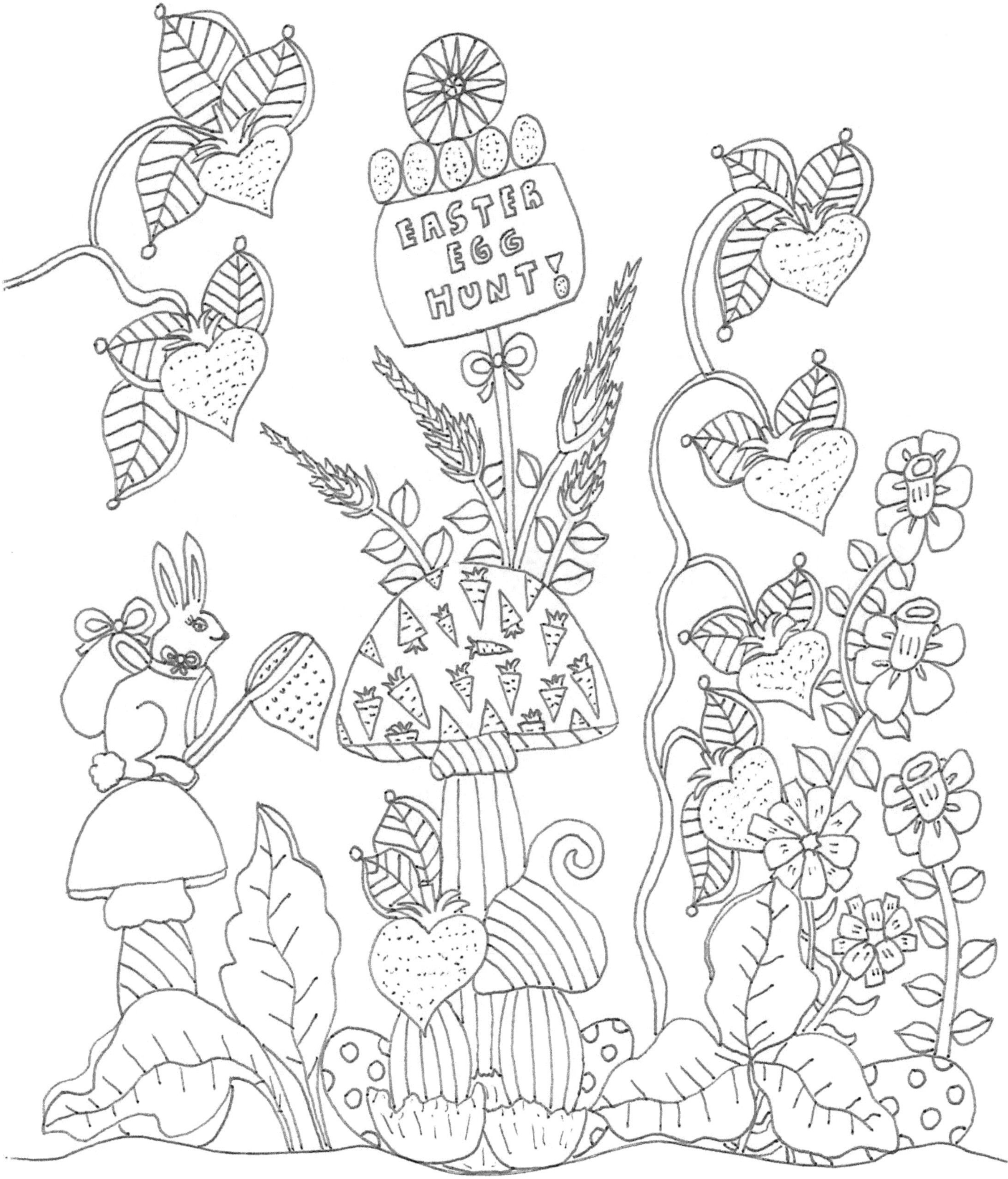
EASTER
EGG
HUNT!

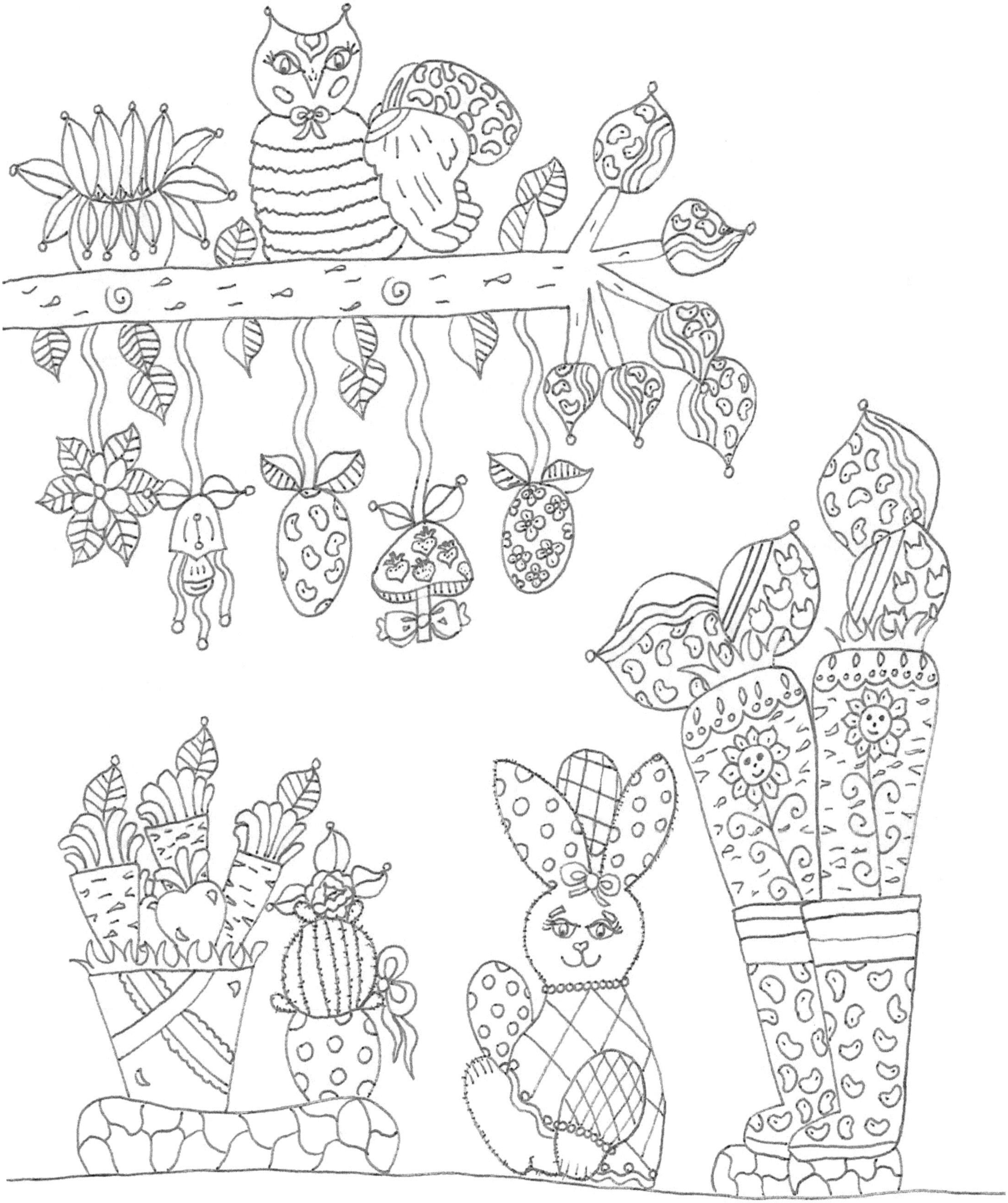

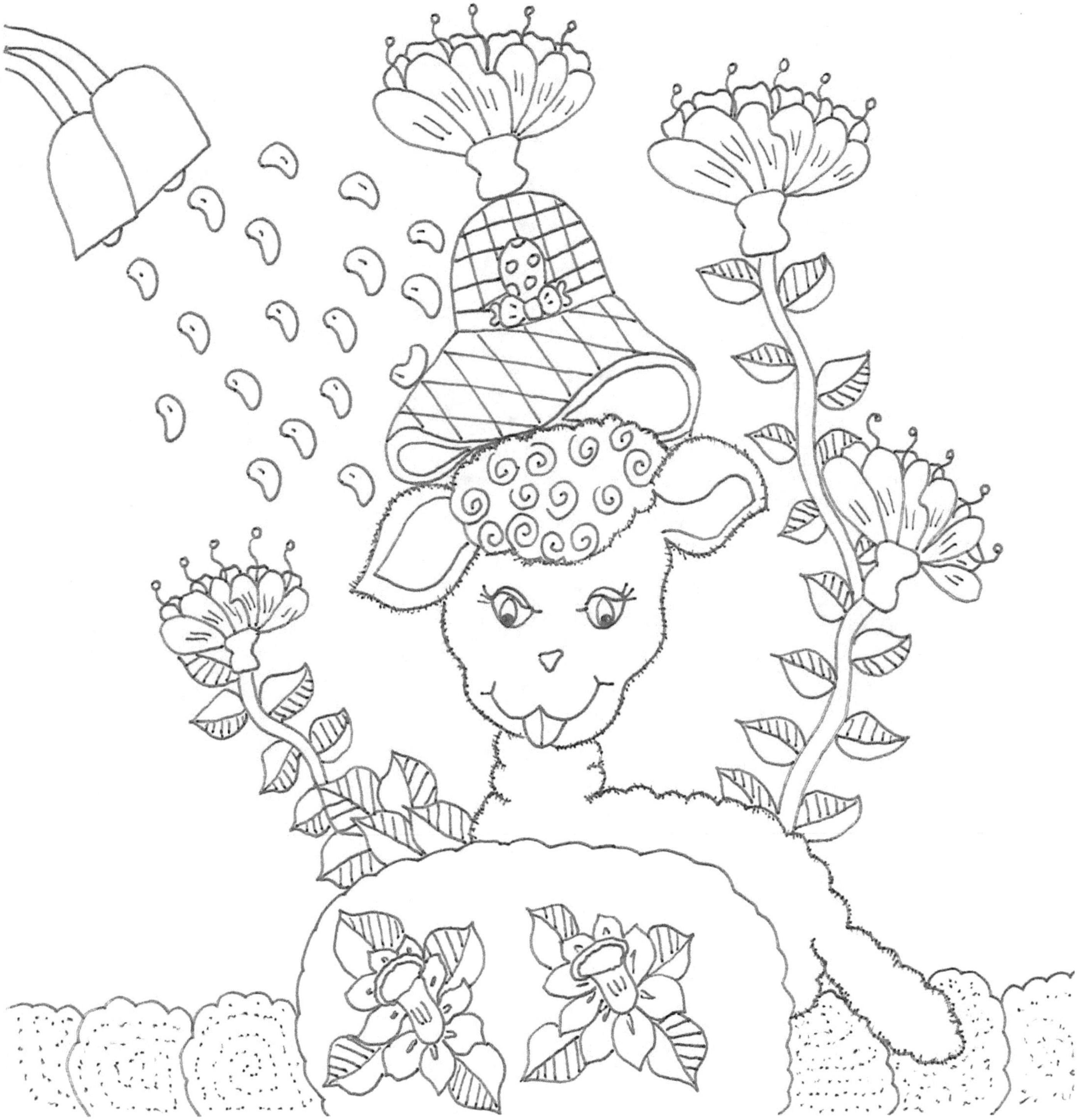

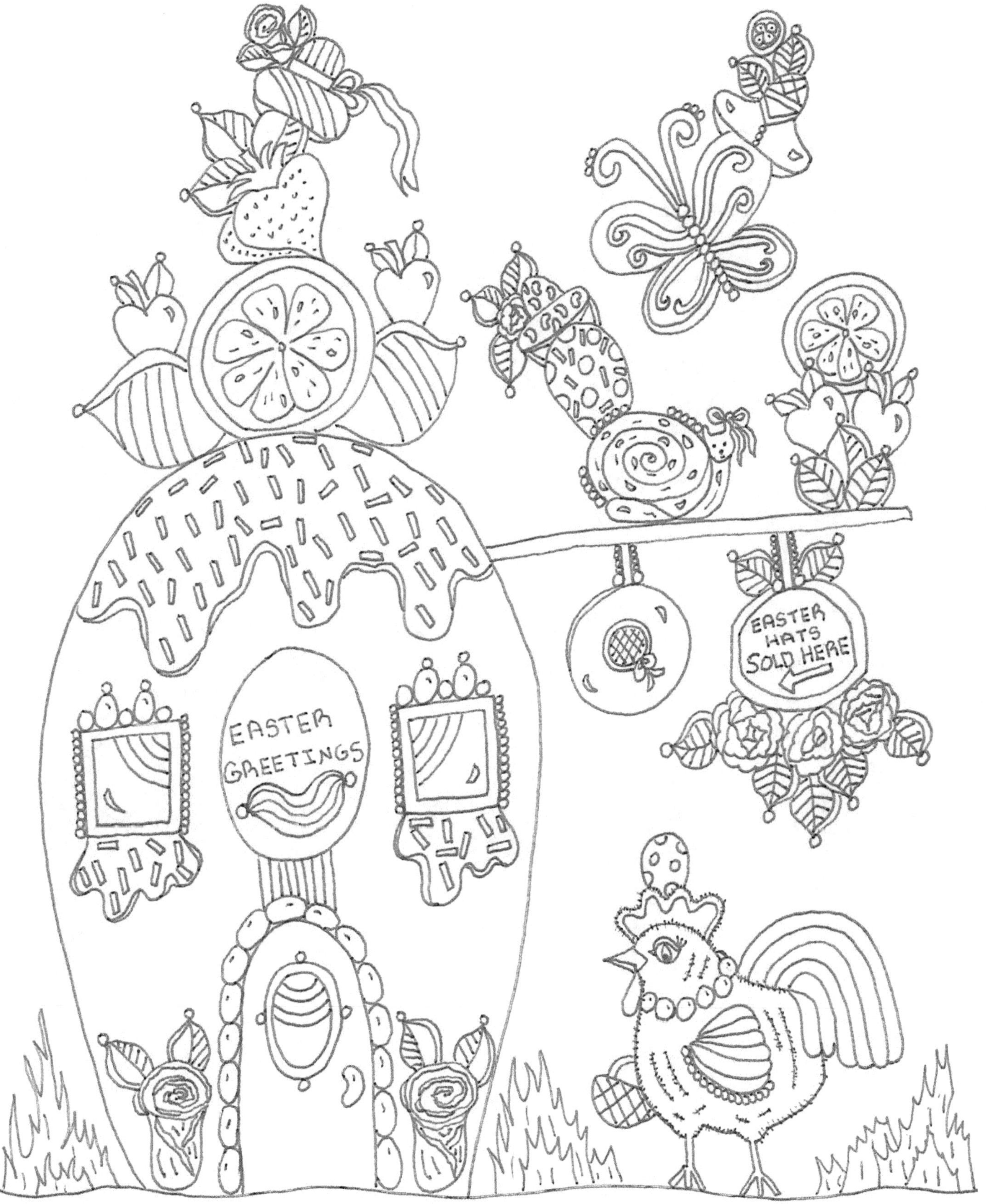
EASTER HATS SOLD HERE
EASTER GREETINGS

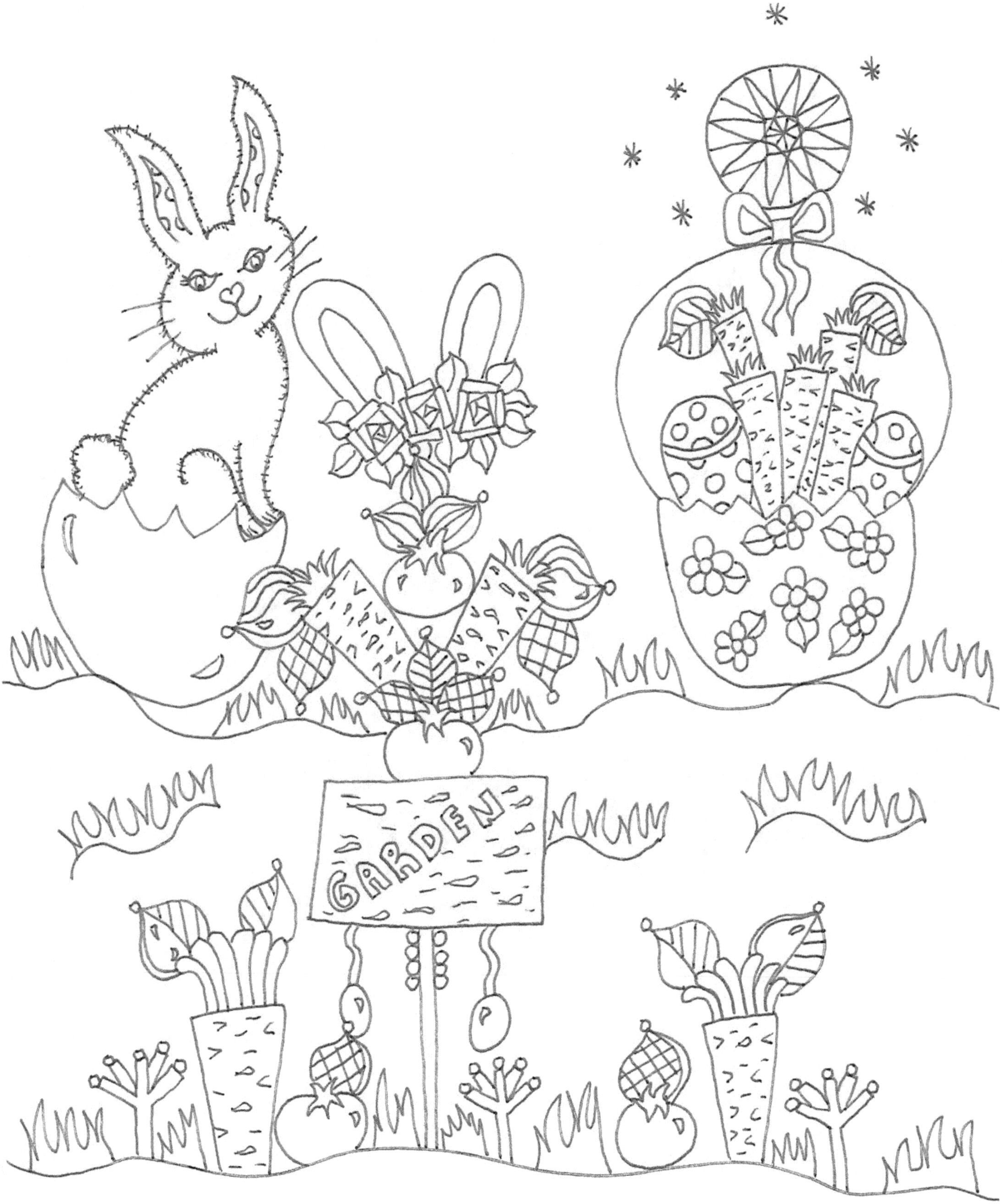
GARDEN

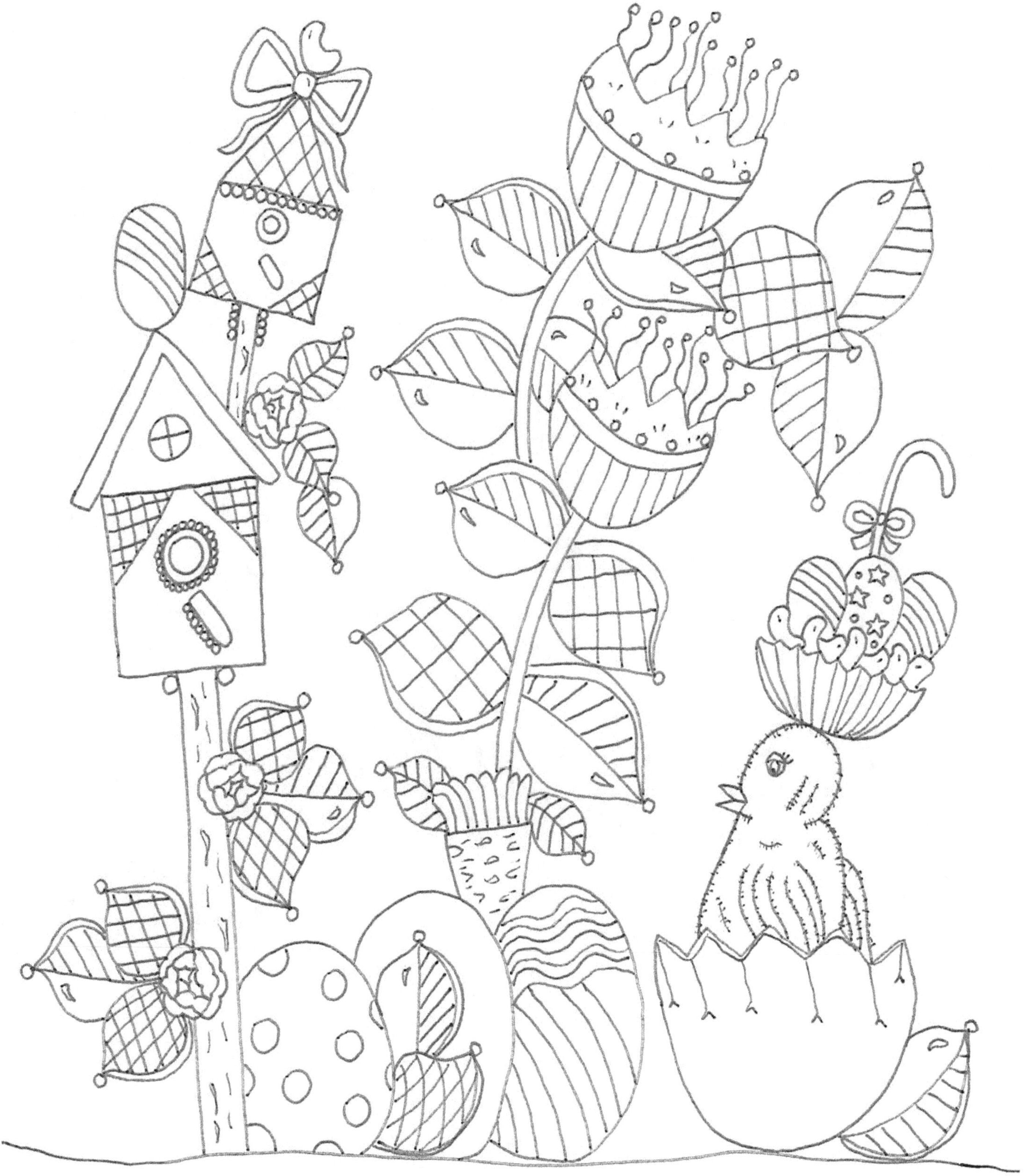

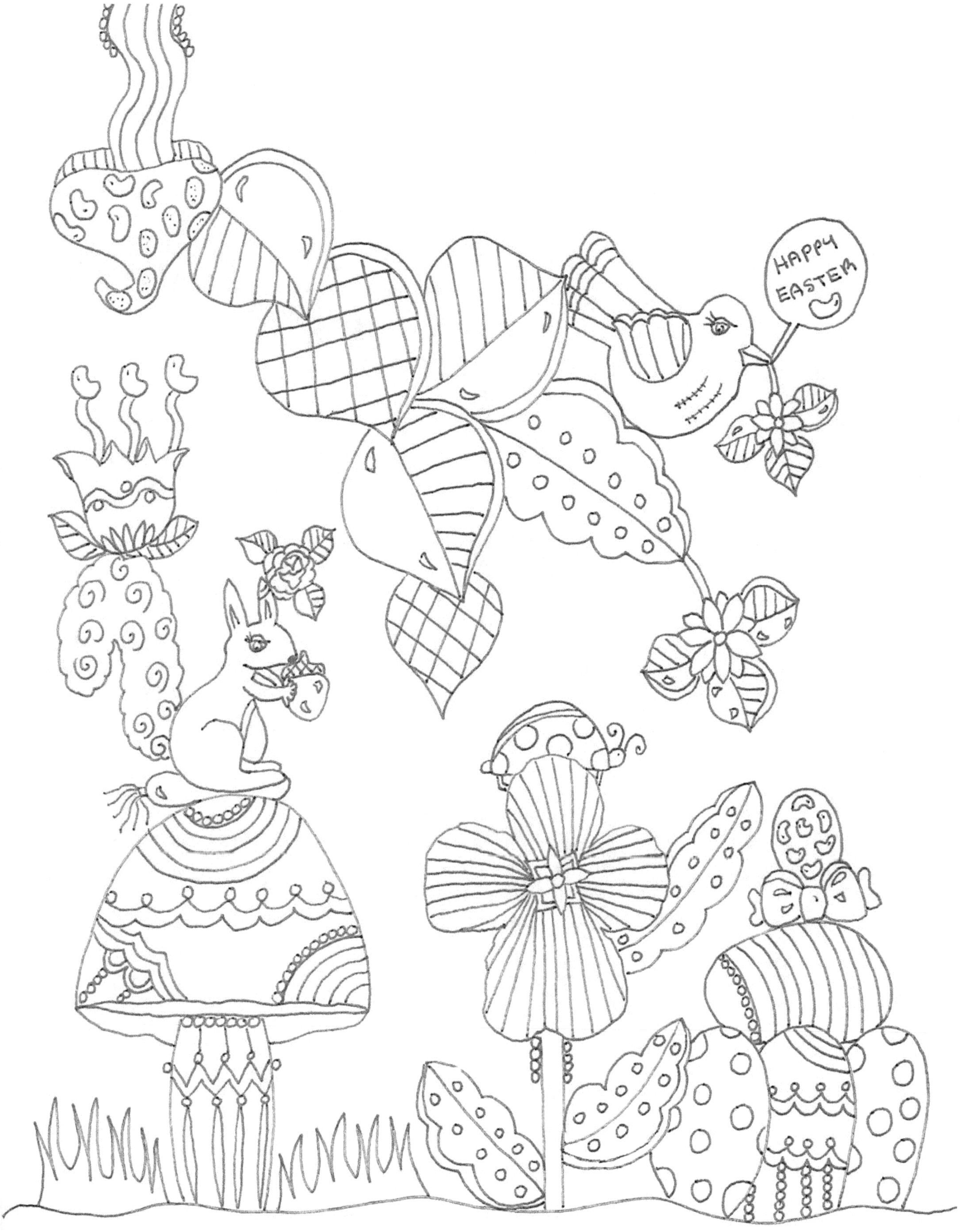
HAPPY
EASTER

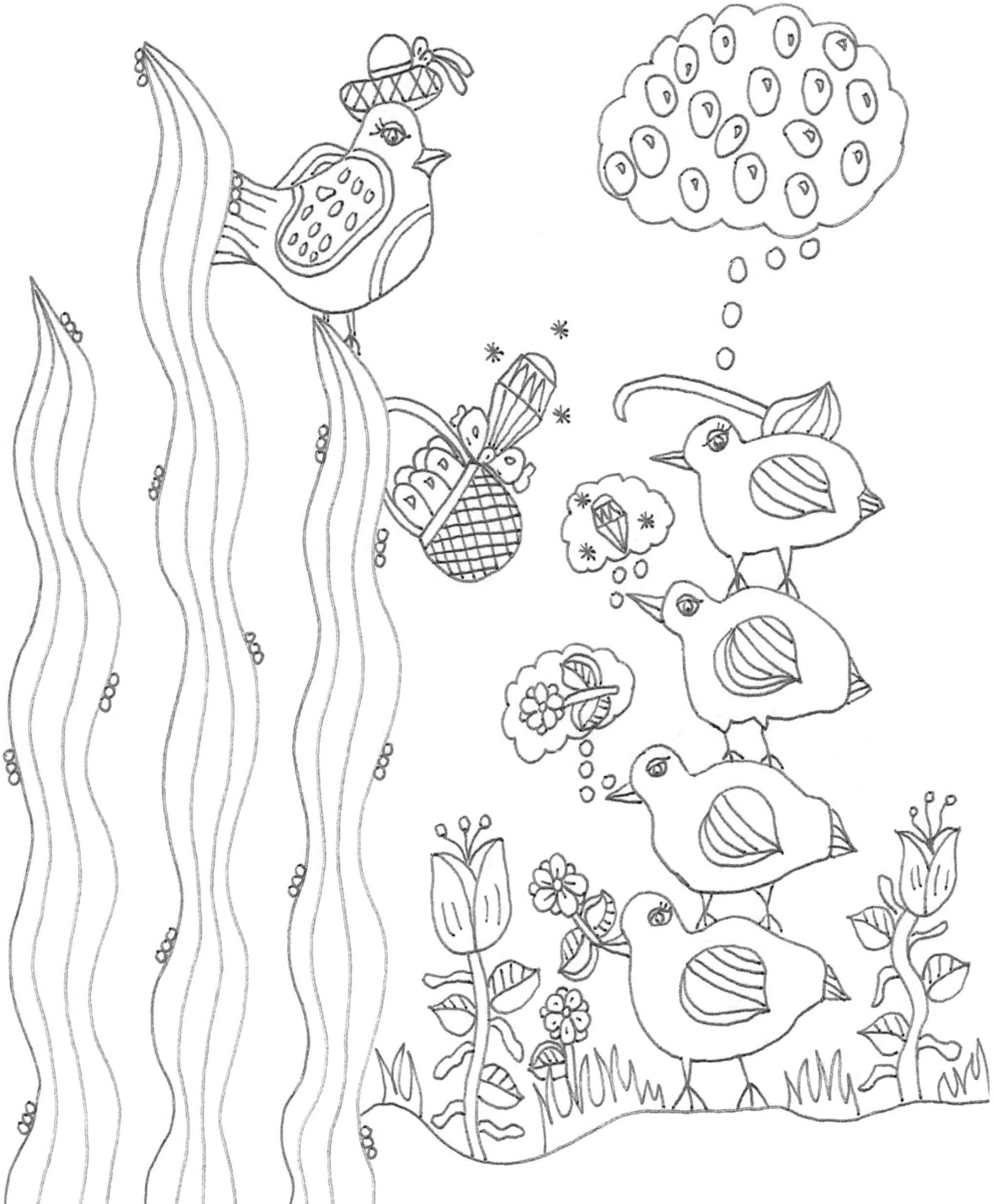

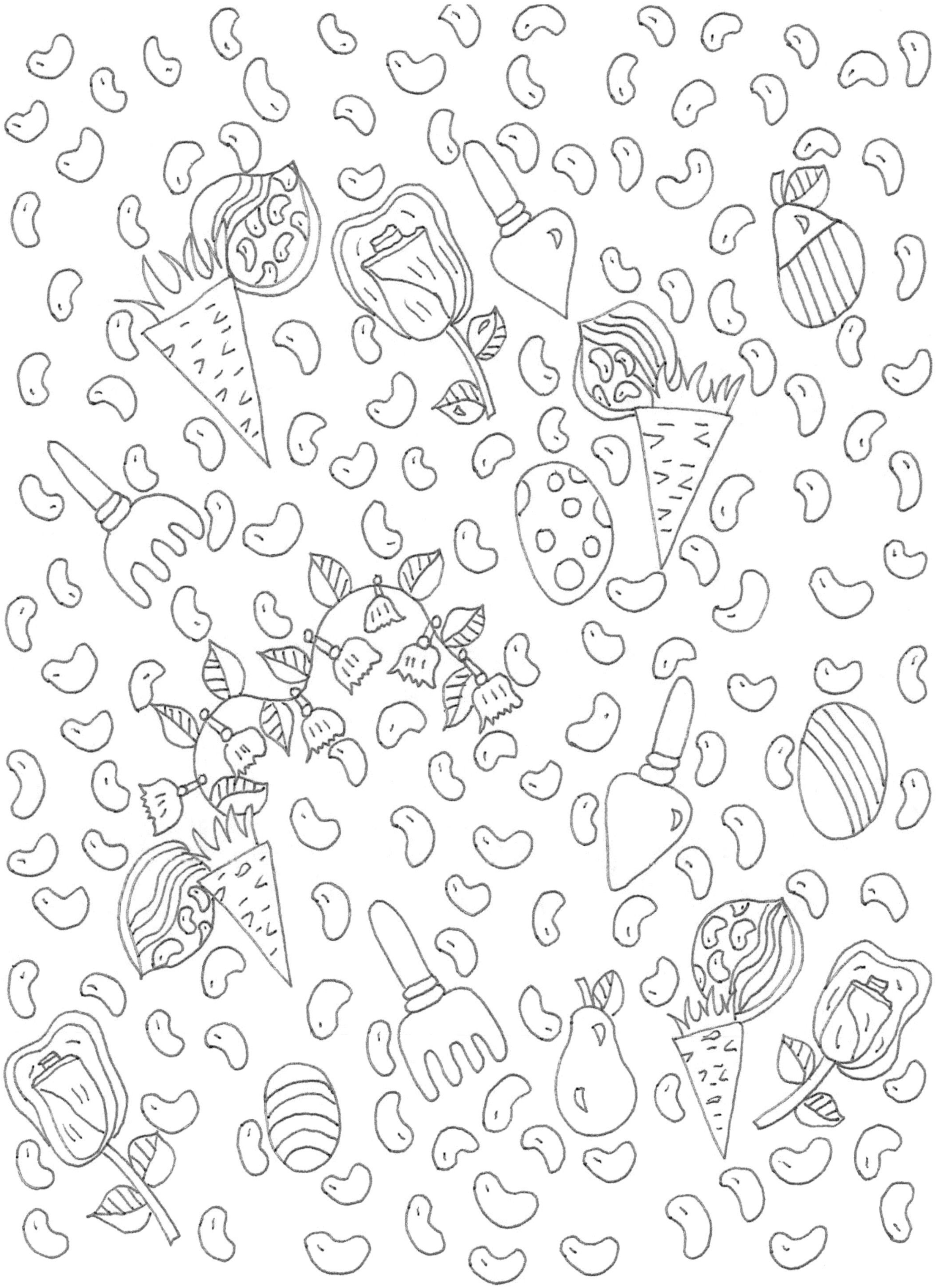

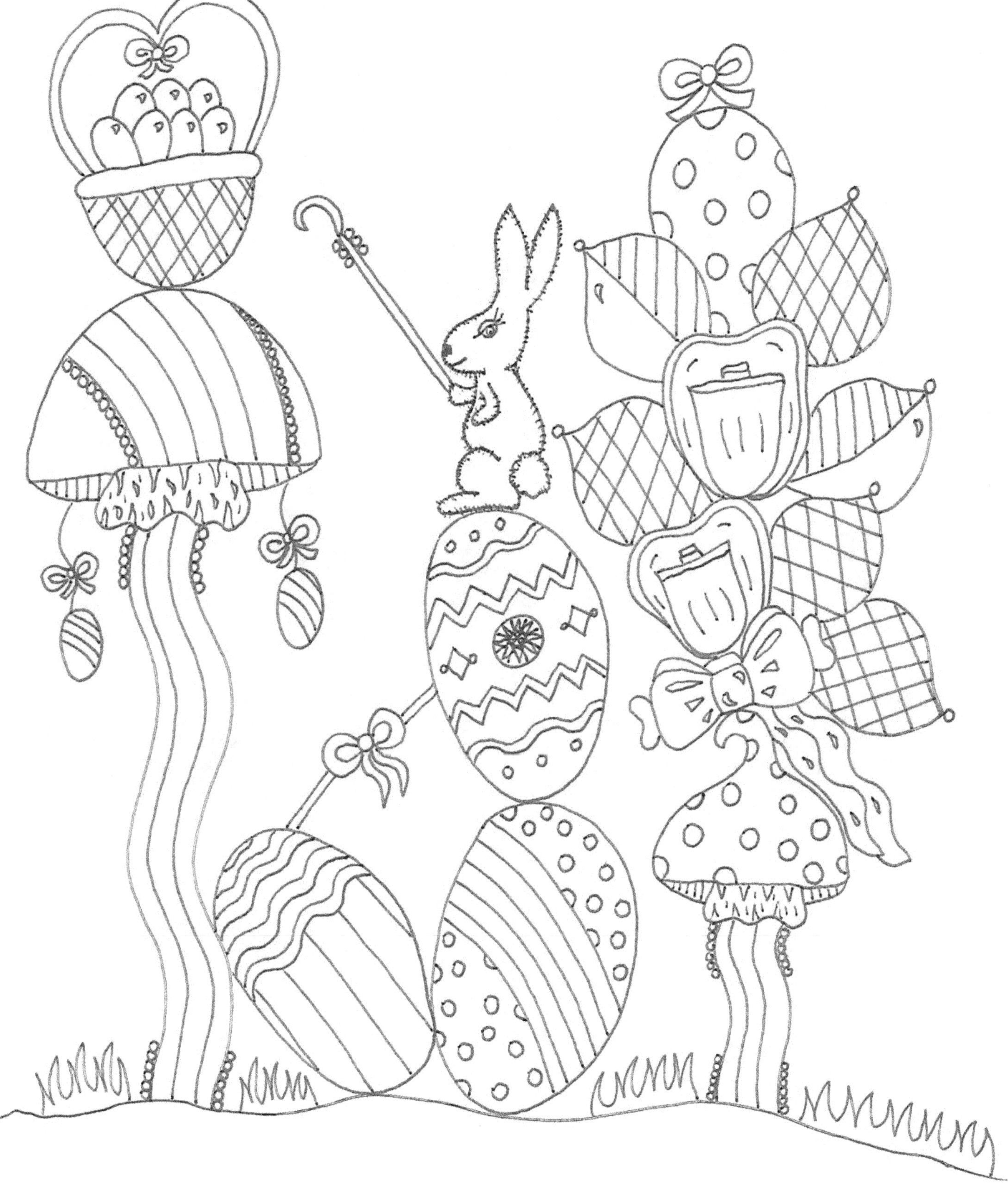

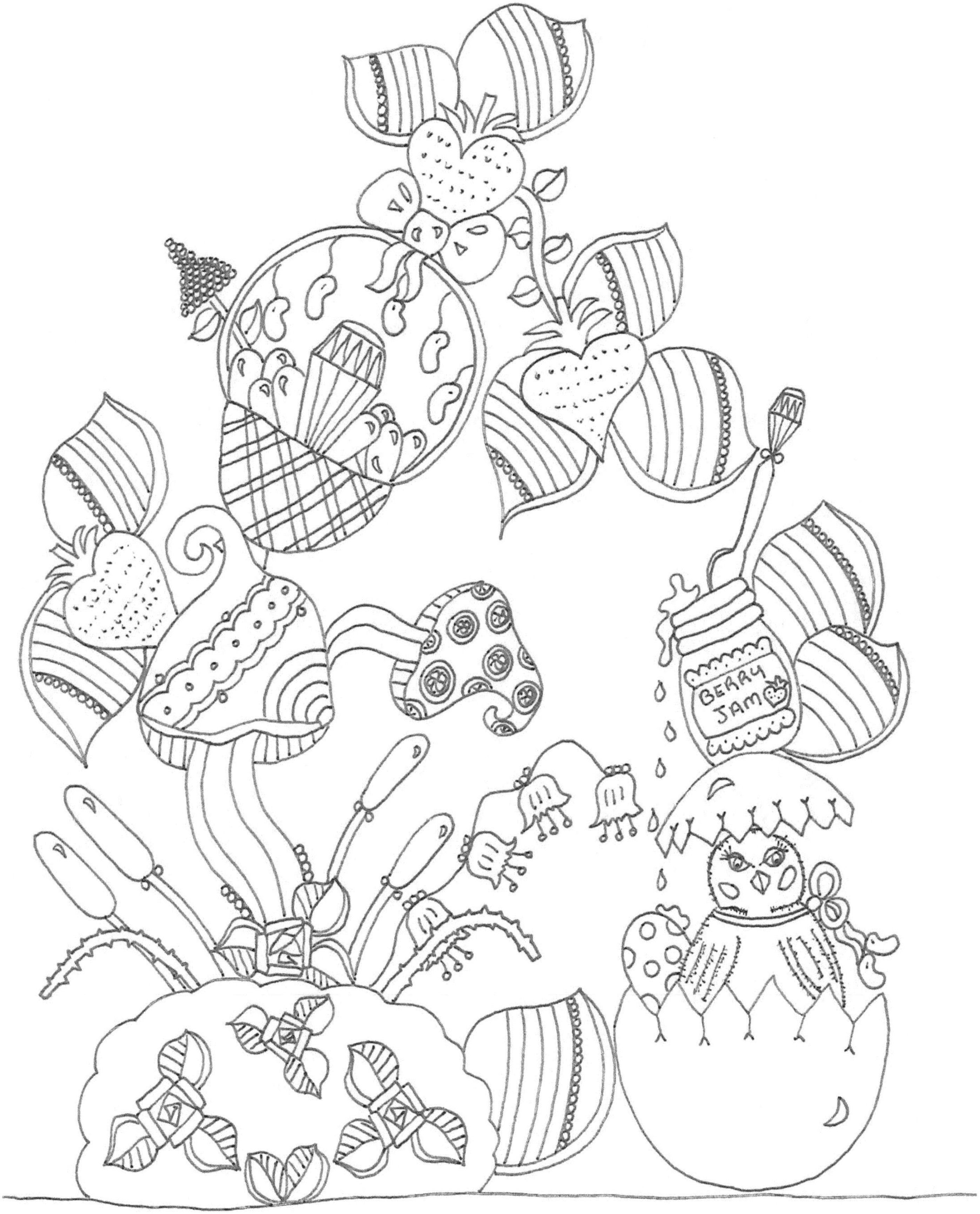
BERRY JAM

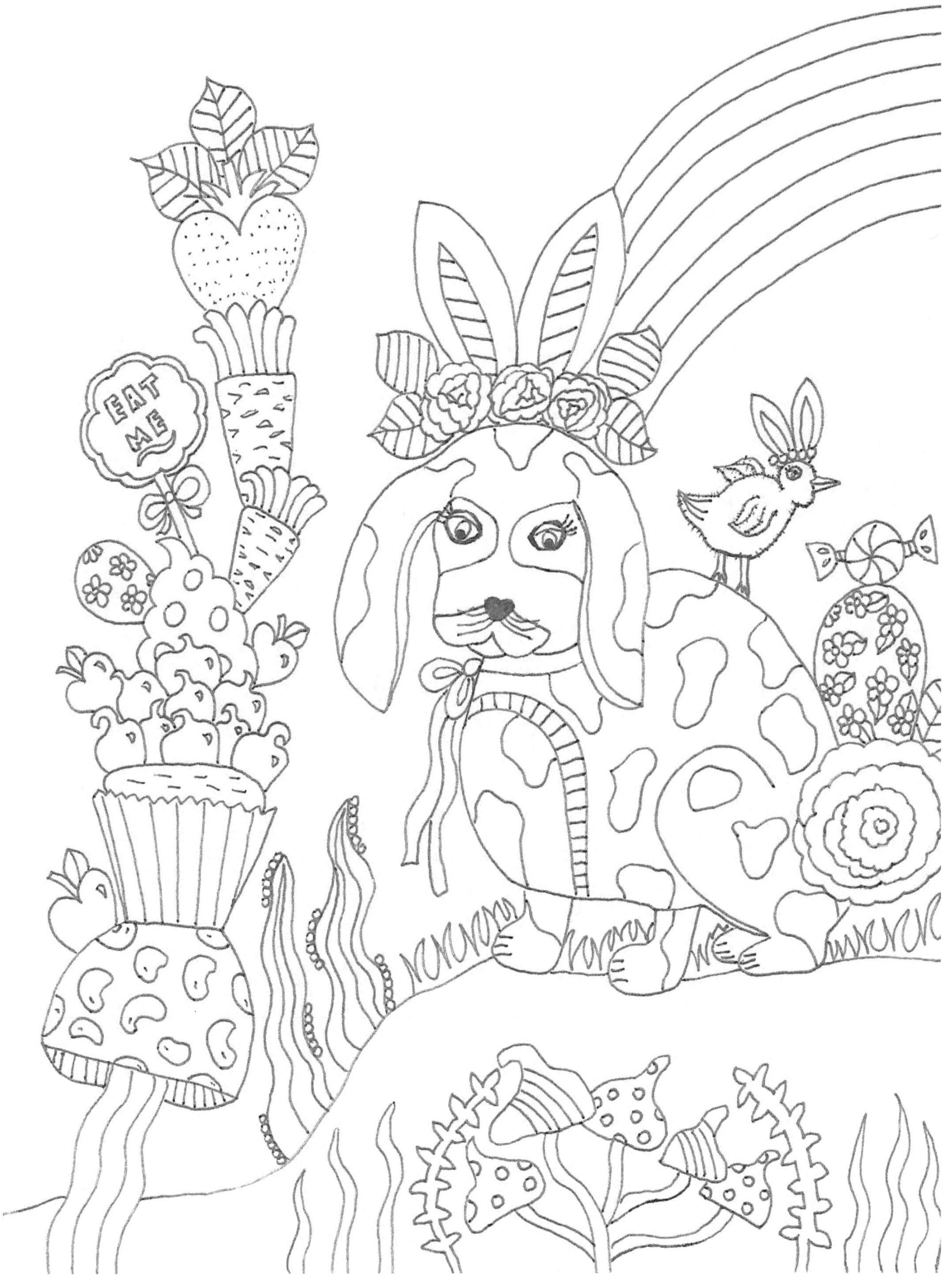
EAT ME

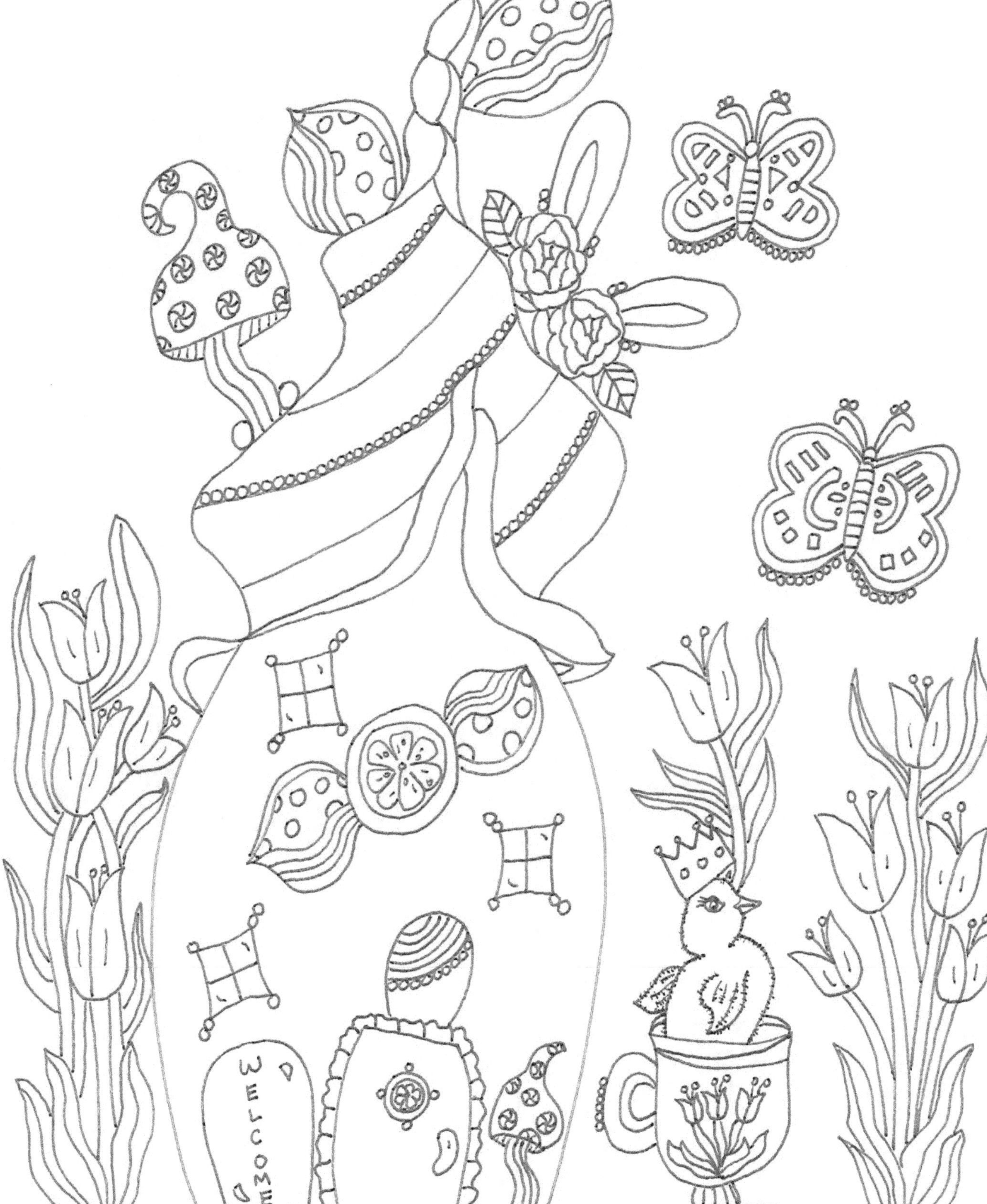
WELCOME

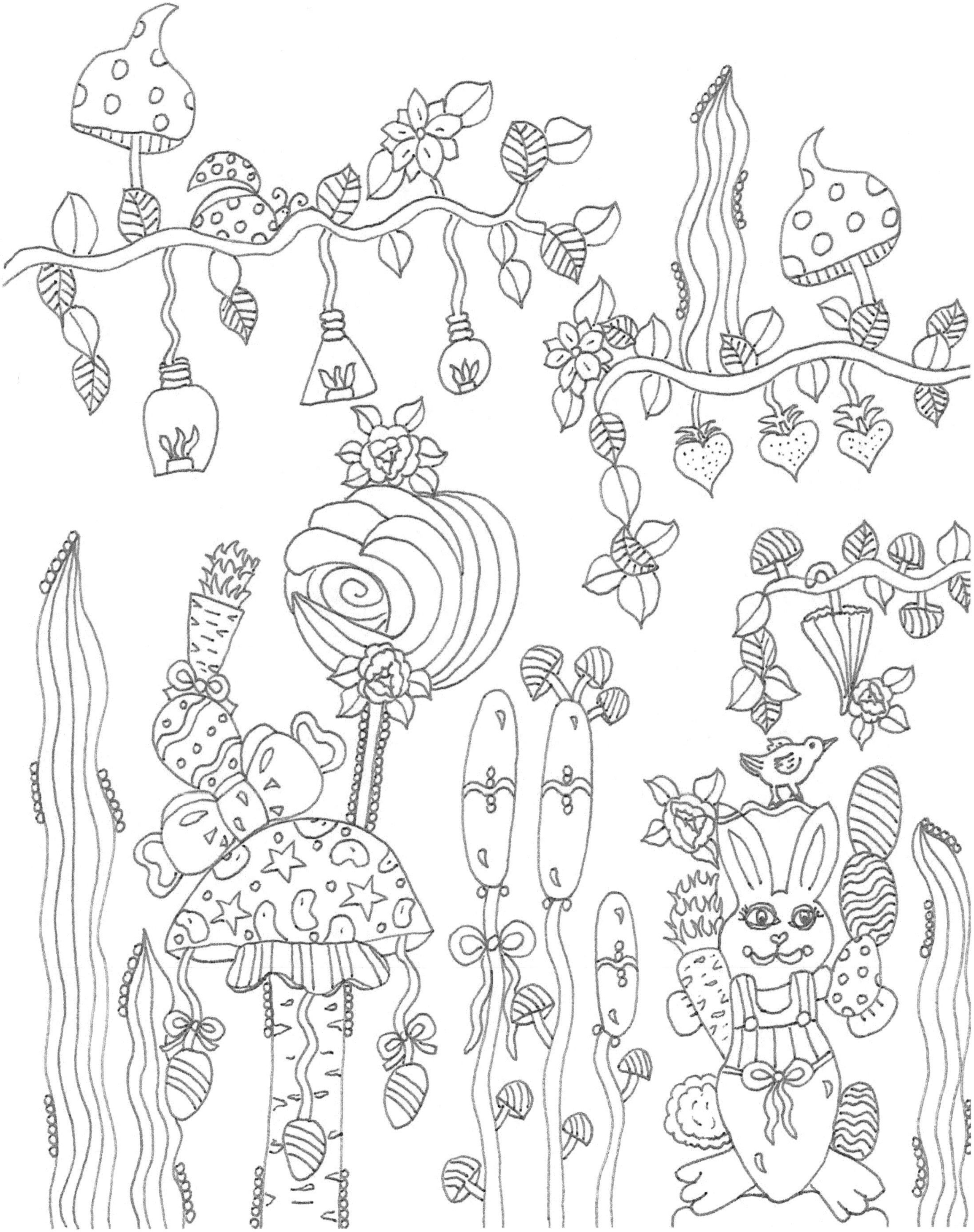

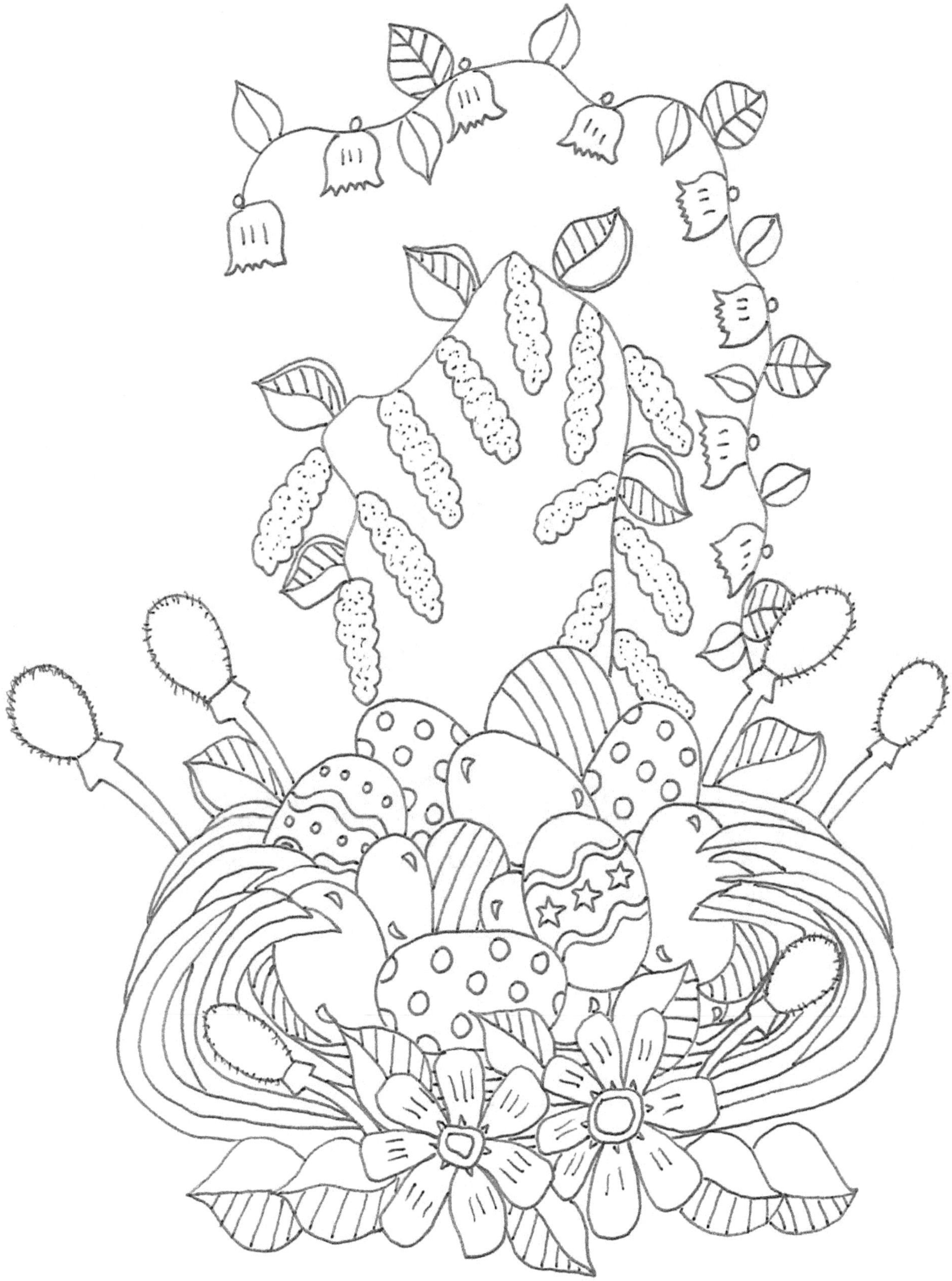

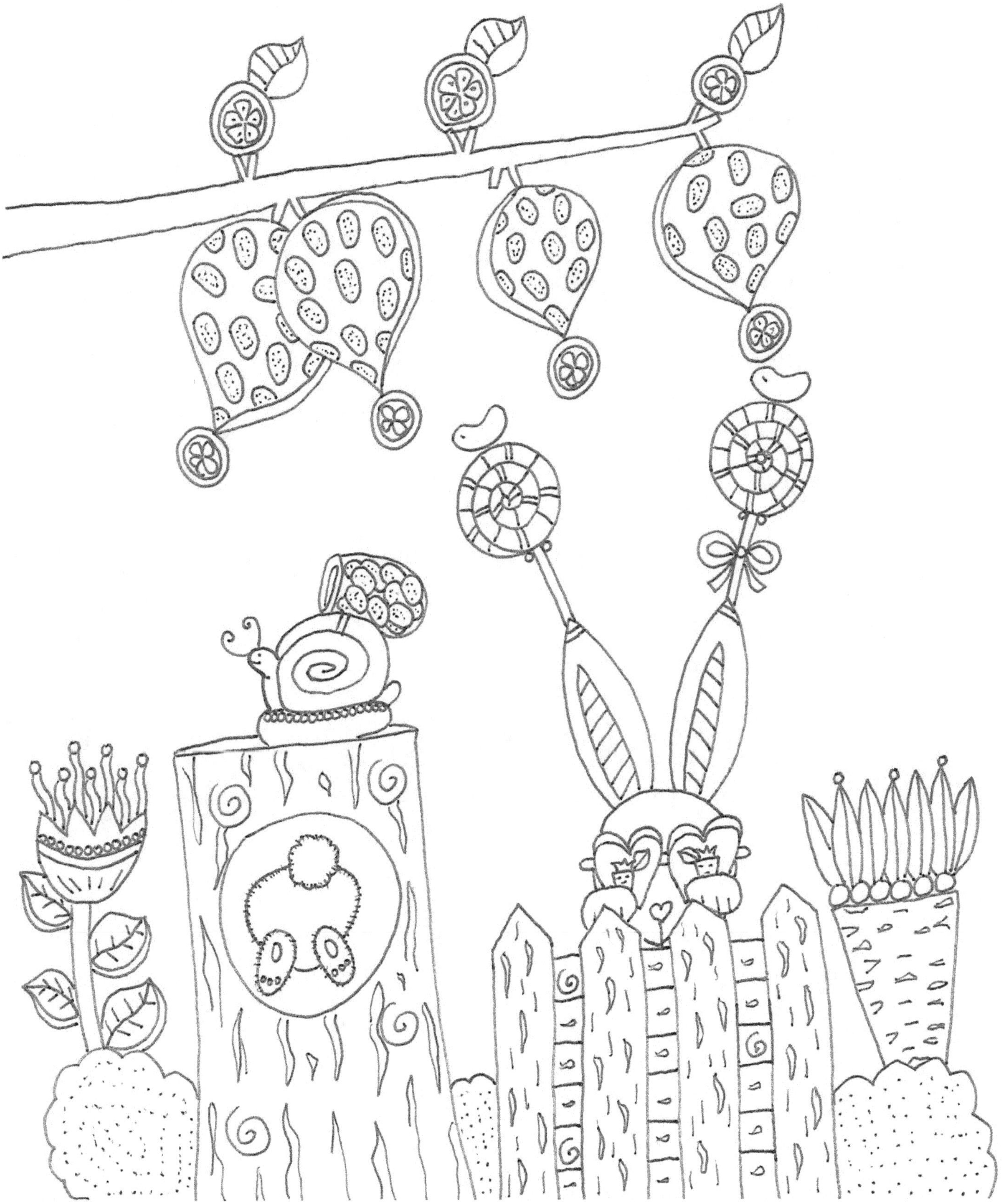

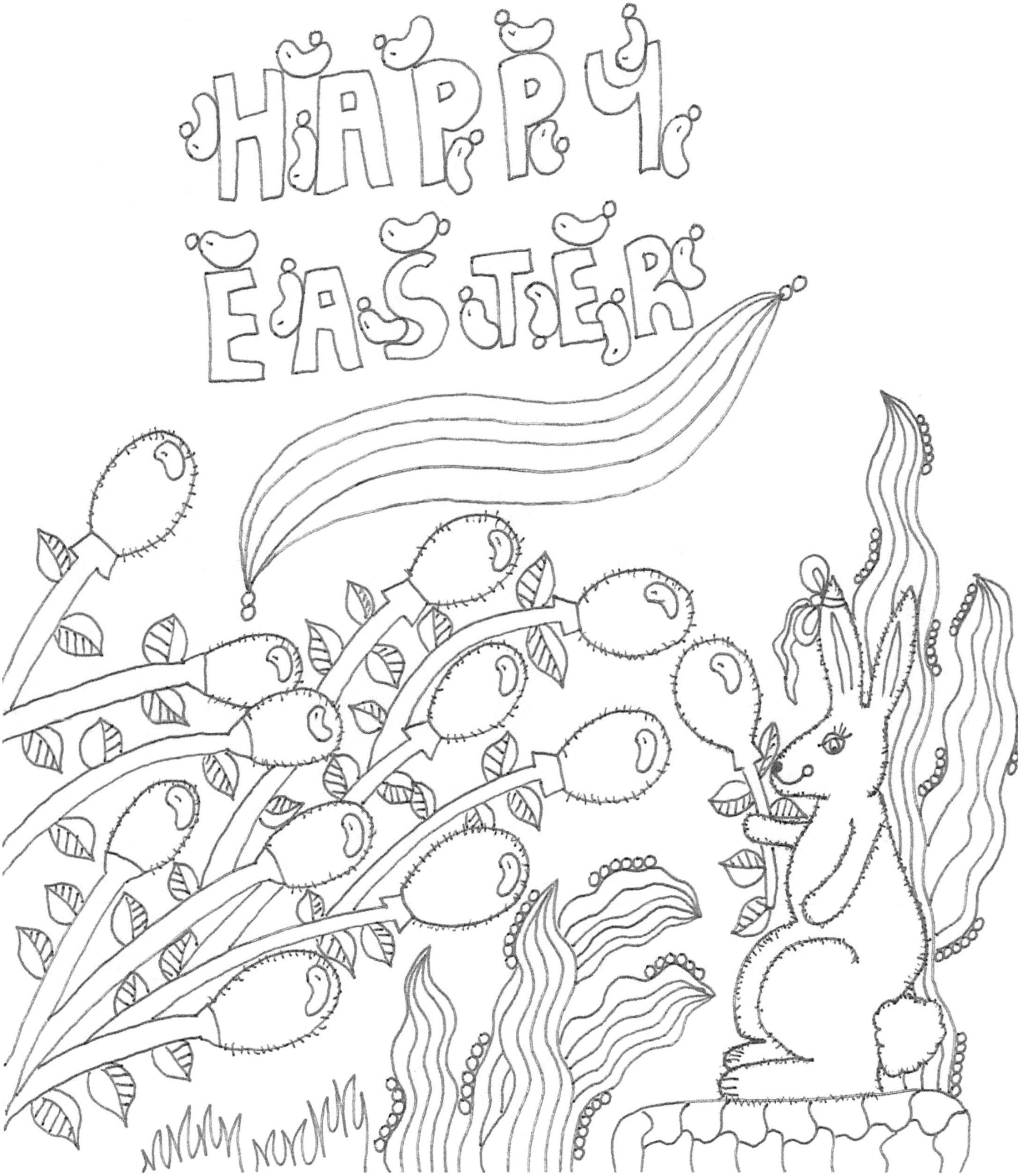

HAPPY
EASTER

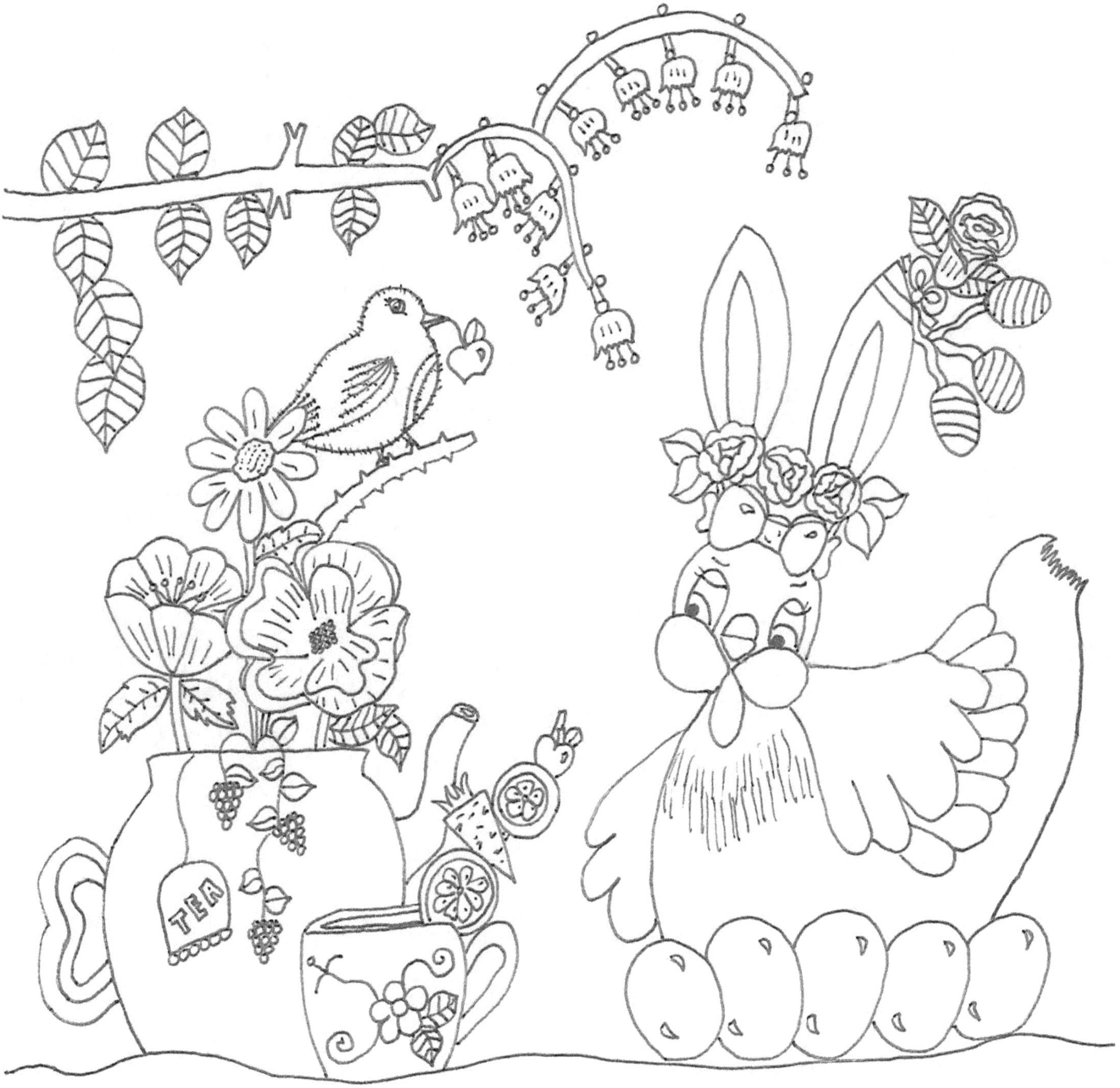
TEA

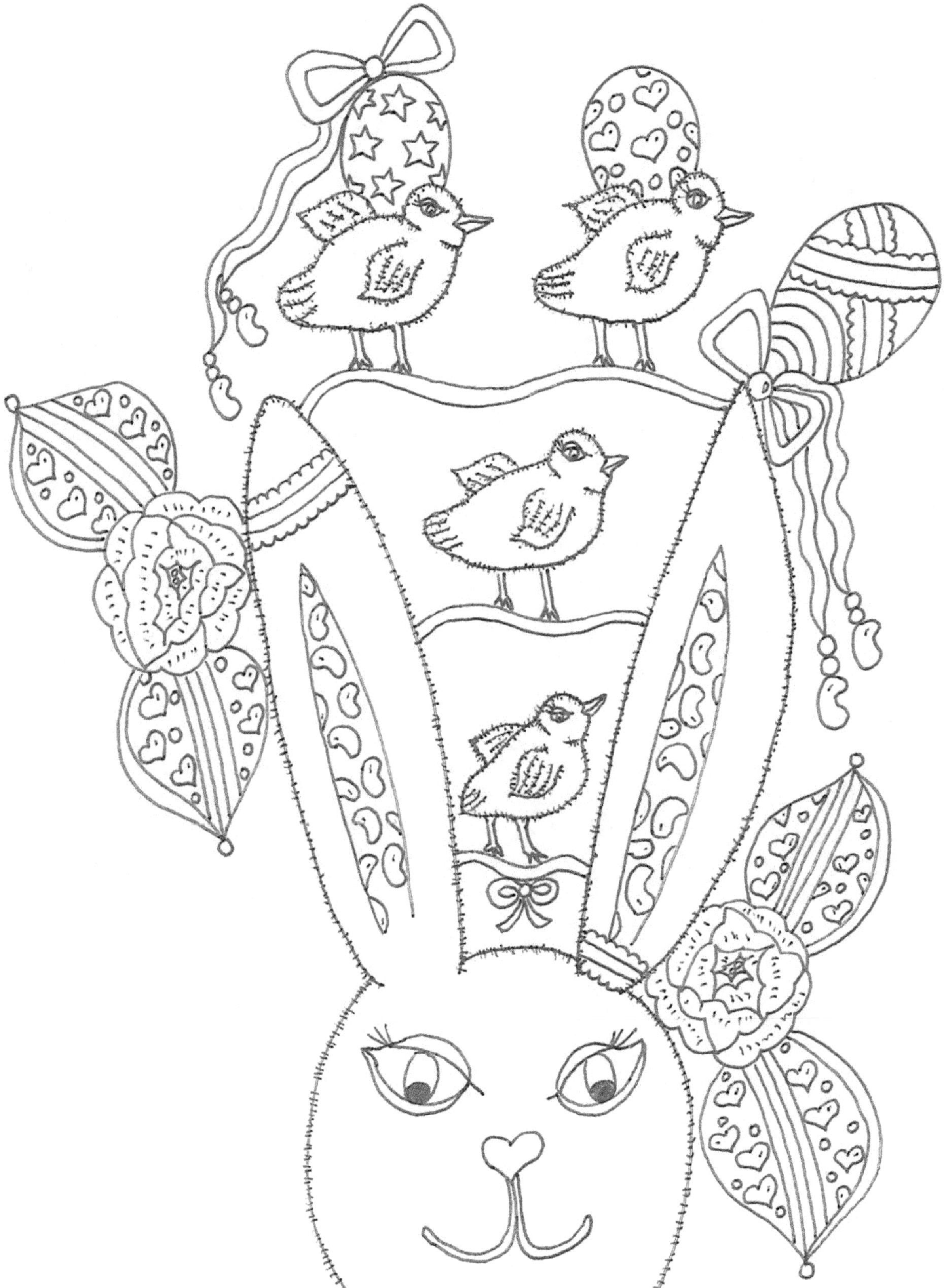

THANK YOU FOR PURCHASING EASTER WONDERLAND ADULT COLORING BOOK. YOU CAN CHECK OUT MY OTHER COLORING BOOKS LISTED BELOW WHICH CAN BE PURCHASED AT AMAZON.COM:

VINTAGE PARIS BAKE SHOP (Adult)
VINTAGE WINE GARDEN (Adult)
ICE CREAM MADNESS (Adult)
ICE CREAM MADNESS VOLUME 2 (Adult)
TEA & COFFEE TROPICAL TREASURES (Adult)
TEA & COFFEE OCEAN TREASURES (Adult)
TEA & COFFEE TREASURES (Adult)
BOTANICAL FLOWERS & MANDALAS (Adult)
MAJESTIC FALL (Adult)
A VERY RETRO CHRISTMAS (Adult)
MAGICAL DESSERTS (Kids)
MAGICAL DESSERTS VOLUME 2 (Kids)
MAGICAL DESSERTS VOLUME 3 (Kids)
FASHION DOLLS (Adult)
FAIRIES IN THE FLOWER GARDEN (Adult)
MERMAID'S WONDERLAND SEA OF ENCHANTMENT (Adult)
CHRISTMAS DESSERTS
VALENTINE'S DAYDREAMS COLORING BOOK (Adult)
VALENTINE'S DAY DELIGHTS (Adult)
VALENTINE'S FLOWERS & DESSERTS (Adult)
VALENTINE'S DAY DESSERTS (Adult)
VALENTINE'S DAY ANIMALS & Sweets (Kids)
VALENTINE DAY'S FLOWERS (Adult)
A VERY RUSTIC VALENTINE'S DAY (Adult)
ELEGANT FLOWERS (Adult)
ST. PATRICK'S DAY BLESSINGS (Adult)
A HAPPY ST. PATTY'S DAY (Kids)
ST. PATRICK'S DAY DESSERTS (Adult)
ST. PATRICK DAY FLOWERS (Adult)
SPRINGTIME FAIRIES (Adult)
SPECTACULAR DESSERTS (Adult)
BEAUTIFUL SPRINGTIME FLOWERS (Adult)
MERMAID DESSERTS (Adult)
FLORAL DELIGHTS (Adult)
FABULOUS SPRINGTIME WREATHS (Adult)
DELICIOUS SPRINGTIME DESSERTS (Adult)
CHARMING EASTER FLOWERS (Adult)

IF YOU ENJOYED YOUR COLORING EXPERIENCE, PLEASE TELL OTHERS ABOUT IT BY WRITING A REVIEW ON AMAZON.COM UNDER THE BOOK YOU COLORED

www.ingramcontent.com/pod-product-compliance
Lightning Source LLC
Chambersburg PA
CBHW080842170526
45158CB00009B/2611
* 9 7 8 1 0 9 0 9 9 5 5 2 0 *